Alan Bitar

Why do you buy?

Alan Bitar

Why do you buy?

What attributes stimulate a consumer to make a choice?

ScienciaScripts

Imprint
Any brand names and product names mentioned in this book are subject to trademark, brand or patent protection and are trademarks or registered trademarks of their respective holders. The use of brand names, product names, common names, trade names, product descriptions etc. even without a particular marking in this work is in no way to be construed to mean that such names may be regarded as unrestricted in respect of trademark and brand protection legislation and could thus be used by anyone.

Cover image: www.ingimage.com

This book is a translation from the original published under ISBN 978-613-9-68203-4.

Publisher:
Sciencia Scripts
is a trademark of
Dodo Books Indian Ocean Ltd. and OmniScriptum S.R.L publishing group

120 High Road, East Finchley, London, N2 9ED, United Kingdom
Str. Armeneasca 28/1, office 1, Chisinau MD-2012, Republic of Moldova, Europe
Printed at: see last page
ISBN: 978-620-8-19676-9

1 INTRODUCTION

The larger a country's economy, the greater people's purchasing power and, consequently, the transfer of the execution of activities to service providers. In this context, Mesquita (2004) defines services as a transaction between individuals, established by an act, an action, an effort or a performance and which can enable the associated transfer of a certain good.

Services are intangible, inseparable, perishable and heterogeneous. Intangible, because they cannot be touched. Inseparable, because they cannot be separated from their suppliers. Perishable, as they should not be stored for sale. Heterogeneous, because they are provided by different people at different times (CHURCHILL JR.; PETER, 2012).

The indirect distribution of services became possible because products were developed that added tangibility to the service. This allowed the use of intermediaries, since some services were separated from the producers. Among the intermediaries, retailers stand out (PETER; DONNELLY Jr., 2013).

Peter and Donnelly Jr. (2013) classify retail as establishments that sell to end consumers. Retailers vary not only in the types of merchandise they work with, but also in the breadth and depth of their product assortments and the amount of services they make available to consumers.

In Brazil, the main types of retailers are traditional and self-service. Traditional retailers are establishments with salespeople or clerks. Self-service retailers are stores with a *check-out* counter at the exit of the store, a cash register and some other equipment that enables the goods to be added up and checked), trolleys or baskets for consumers to 'self-serve' (CHURCHILL JR.; PETER, 2012).

Among self-service stores, hypermarkets and supermarkets stand out for their ability to sell a variety of products: dry groceries, liquid groceries, electronics, imports and organic products. Other supermarkets have a variety of businesses, such as agribusiness, gas stations, snack bars, restaurants and pharmacies (FGV, 2011).

Retail activities are fundamental to a country's economy, as they provide jobs for the population and generate high tax revenues. They also bring benefits to suppliers and buyers.

As far as suppliers are concerned, the retail trade offers an efficient way of making goods available to consumers. As for buyers, retail allows for a diversity of products, in convenient quantities and at appropriate times (CHURCHILL JR.; PETER, 2012).

According to the Brazilian Association of Supermarkets - ABRAS (2017b), in June 2017 the

Brazilian retail trade grew by 1.2% in sales volume and 0.8% in nominal revenue, both compared to the previous month (series free of seasonal influences). The results were considered the third consecutive positive rate in this comparison.

In terms of sales volume, the sectors that stood out the most were textiles, clothing and footwear (5.4%); books, newspapers, magazines and stationery (4.5%); other personal and household articles (2.7%); furniture and household appliances (2.2%); pharmaceutical, medical, orthopaedic, perfumery and cosmetic articles (1.5%); and fuels and lubricants (1.2%) (ABRAS, 2017b).

On the other hand, there was a drop in the hypermarkets, supermarkets, food products, beverages and tobacco segments, with a decrease of 0.4%, after a 1.1% increase in May and 1.3% in April. However, in July of the same year, real sales in the supermarket sector rose by 4.21% compared to June, according to the National Sales Index calculated by ABRAS (2017b).

In nominal terms, sales in the supermarket sector rose in July 2017, with a variation of 4.46% compared to the previous month (ABRAS, 2017b).

When comparing the retail sales volume rate in June 2017 (1.2%) with the same month a year earlier, the retail trade grew by 3.0% in 2016. It was the third positive result on this basis of comparison and more intense than the months of May (2.6%) and April (1.7%) of the respective year. Sectorally speaking, the segments that contributed most were furniture and household appliances (12.7%); fabrics, clothing and footwear (4.6%); other personal and household articles (4.3%); pharmaceutical, medical, orthopaedic and perfumery articles (3.0%); and books, newspapers, magazines and stationery (1.2%) (ABRAS, 2017b).

From another perspective, the sectors that contributed the least were hypermarkets, supermarkets, food products, beverages and tobacco, with 0.8%, after growth of 3.0% in April; followed by fuels and lubricants, with 0.5% (ABRAS, 2017b).

As in 2016, 2017 also presented a challenging scenario in the hypermarket and supermarket sectors, as families began to adopt new measures with regard to consumption. A study carried out by Nielsen Consulting (2016) highlighted that many Brazilian families have become more attentive to their shopping carts, have become open to switching brands, have rationed the month's purchases and have prioritized products that deliver a good cost-benefit ratio.

In a context such as the current one, in which unemployment affects more than thirteen million economically active Brazilians, it can be seen that this concern has become part of the daily lives of consumers and also of the retail trade, especially the supermarket segment (ABRAS, 2017b).

For Mesquita (2004), the supermarket sector, as it is a competitive environment, needs to create critical resources to meet consumer needs. The company needs to organize itself so that customers find total satisfaction and achieve what they want, because if it doesn't, the company could lose the customer to a competitor.

Faced with this scenario in which the pace of economic recovery is still slow, the hypermarket and supermarket segments are facing an increasingly competitive environment, with greater competition for consumer resources and even more demanding and unfaithful customers.

In this context, price is an important factor in the competitive environment, but it is not the only factor to consider. Peter and Donnelly Jr. (2013) highlight other attributes such as promotion. From this perspective, Mesquita (2004) elucidates that price is no longer a key attribute and concerns related to sales promotion and, above all, how to get sales appear.

1.1 Problem

Changes in the consumer market have required supermarket retailers to pay more attention to aspects such as layout, product advertising and customer service, among others.

Specifically in the municipality of Palmas-TO, there have been recent changes. In 1989, the year the capital of Tocantins was founded, the area was uninhabited and had no infrastructure, but over time, stores began to appear; offices; small, family-run supermarkets, where the shopkeeper knew the consumer's habits and called them by name; among other establishments.

Medium to large supermarkets began to set up in the municipality of Palmas from 1999 onwards, most notably Supermercado Caçulinha and Quartetto Supermercado.

The city of Palmas currently has five large supermarket chains: Quartetto Supermercado; Big Supermercado; Atacadista Atacadao, belonging to the Carrefour Group; Atacadista Makro; and Hipermercado Extra, belonging to the Pao de Açùcar Group.

With the arrival of large supermarket chains in the town, such as Atacadista Atacadao, Atacadista Makro and Hipermercado Extra, consumers have become more demanding and experienced in terms of purchasing, both in terms of information and new shopping experiences.

Based on the above arguments, I came up with the guiding question for this project: What are the main attributes considered by consumers when choosing a supermarket to shop at?

In view of the question posed in this project, the general and specific objectives are presented below.

1.2 General Objective

To describe and analyze the attributes that influence the final consumer's decision-making process when choosing a supermarket in the municipality of Palmas, state of Tocantins.

1.2.1 Specifics

a)   Identify the main attributes that influence the final consumer when choosing a supermarket.

b)   To identify the main attributes that influence final consumers to repurchase in the same supermarket.

1.3 Justification

From an academic point of view, it is believed that this study could contribute to understanding the variables of the marketing mix in the context of the supermarket sector. In order to build the theoretical framework, a search was carried out in the *Scientific Periodicals Electronic Library* (SPELL) database, with a filter from January 2000 to September 2017, involving the title supermarket, and 86 results were found. Specifically, the topics covered relate to various contexts of organizational studies: innovation, marketing, social responsibility, among others. Therefore, it is believed that this research can contribute, especially by analyzing the marketing mix.

In addition to the justifications mentioned here, the work is also justified by contributing to the retail trade, elucidating the characteristics of the sector, explaining its needs, among others.

After describing the study in this introduction, including the problem, the general and specific objectives and the justification, this work is structured into five chapters.

The second chapter reviews the literature based on the following lines of research: consumer behavior; relationship marketing; price and perceived value; and the retail segment. The third chapter looks at the environment, focusing on the retail segment in the municipality of Palmas. In the fourth chapter, the methodology involving the research approach and the data collection technique. The fifth and final chapter presents and analyzes the research data.

2 THEORETICAL FRAMEWORK

The aim of this section is to address the main topics involved in this work and to support the researcher in achieving the objective proposed in the research problem. The following topics were explored: 'Consumer behavior'; 'Relationship marketing'; 'Price and perceived value'; and 'Retail segment'.

2.1 Consumer Behavior

Consumer behavior is a much-studied topic in marketing theory, emphasizing demographic characteristics and issues pertaining to consumer attitudes and needs, thus integrating concepts from the sciences of human behavior (SOLOMON, 2016).

Solomon (2016, p. 06) defines consumer behavior as "a study of the processes involved when individuals or groups select, buy, use or discard products, services, ideas or experiences to satisfy needs and desires".

Churchill Jr. and Peter (2012) illustrate consumer behavior as the feelings, thoughts and actions of buyers and the influences on them that produce certain changes.

Sheth, Mittal and Newman (2001) define consumer behavior as mental, physical and social activities carried out by consumers that result in decisions and actions to buy, pay for or use products and services.

Larentis (2009) explains that mental activities are those related to information processing and product decision-making; physical activities refer to travel, energy expenditure and physical effort; and social activities are those related to interactions between individuals in the process of acquisition, use and disposal.

According to Goldstein and Almeida (2000), various models have been created to describe consumer behavior and, for didactic purposes, the models have been divided into stimulus-reaction and explanatory. Stimulus-reaction models are mathematical and seek to predict the reaction of a system to a given stimulus. Explanatory models aim to understand the reasons that lead consumers to make a decision, thus explaining their behavior.

Explanatory models are the pillars of consumer behavior theory and their relevance goes beyond the simple approach of their ability to predict one situation or another (GOLDSTEIN; ALMEIDA, 2000).

Authors such as Kotler, McCarthy, Stanton and Holtje identify five phases that represent the consumer buying process: felt need, search for information, evaluation of alternatives, purchase decision and post-purchase feelings. These phases gave rise to integrative explanatory theories such as: the Engel, Blackwell and Miniard model; the Howard-Sheth model; the Nicosia model; the Sheth, Mittal and Newman model; the Howard model; among others (GOLDSTEIN; ALMEIDA, 2000).

Goldstein and Almeida (2000) describe three models of consumer behavior as the most comprehensive and complete: Engel, Blackwell and Miniard, Howard-Sheth and Nicosia. However, this project will focus on the Engel, Blackwell and Miniard, Howard-Sheth and Nicosia models, as they are the most comprehensive, and the Sheth, Mittal and Newman model, as it is the most innovative.

In Engel, Blackwell and Miniard's model, the consumer's decision is influenced by various factors, which are grouped into the following categories: individual differences, environmental influences and psychological processes (ENGEL; BLACKWELL; MINIARD, 2000).

Individual differences include: consumer resources, knowledge, attitude, motivation and personality. Environmental influences include the following variables: culture, social class, personal influence, family and situation. Psychological processes include: information processing, learning, attitude change and behavior (ENGEL; BLACKWELL; MINIARD, 2000).

The central focus of Engel, Blackwell and Miniard's model is on the choice process, which is made up of: recognition of need, search, pre-purchase alternative evaluation, purchase, consumption and results (ENGEL; BLACKWELL; MINIARD, 2000).

The Howard-Sheth model explains the process by which the buyer is transformed by learning mechanisms, by commercial and marketing stimuli (inputs) and also by the reactions caused by these stimuli (outputs) (LOPES; SILVA, 2011).

The model covers four variables involved in the consumer behavior process: input, output, hypothetical constructs and exogenous variables. The input variables represent the social or commercial environment. The output variables display the manifest behavior of the consumer (attention, brand understanding, attitude, intention and purchase). The hypothetical constructs are divided into perception and learning. The exogenous variables describe the context in which consumer behavior occurs (LOPES; SILVA, 2011).

The Nicosia model establishes that buying behavior is preceded by research and evaluation of data and that these are preceded by exposure to a message created by the seller or supplier (LOPES; SILVA, 2011).

In the Sheth, Mittal and Newman model, the individual decision-making process involves decisions such as: what to buy, when, from whom and how to pay. Decisions can be influenced by people who can take on the role of: customer, user or payer (MESQUITA, 2004).

According to Mesquita (2004), Sheth, Mittal and Newman's model is summarized in five phases: problem recognition, information search, evaluation of alternatives, purchase and post-purchase experience.

The next subsection explains some of the concepts pertinent to relationship marketing.

2.2 Relationship Marketing

Relationship marketing is not a new term in management. It was launched around 1980 and its origins are related to the School of Services (SLONGO; MUSSNICH, 2005).

For Stone and Woodcock (1998), relationship marketing is the use of various marketing, sales, communication and customer care techniques and processes to identify individual customers, establish a lasting relationship with them and manage this relationship for the benefit of the company and its customers.

According to Bogmann (2000), relationship marketing is about creating, maintaining and enhancing customer relationships. The author mentions that every day, marketing is shifting its focus from individual transactions to the development of relationships that have value and networks that offer value.

Relationship marketing must enable customer satisfaction. To this end, it has eight main components: cultures and values; leadership; strategy; structure; personnel; technology; knowledge and perception and processes (MONTEIRO, 2003).

Gronroos (2003) explains that relationship marketing represents a paradigm shift in marketing concepts, replacing the focus on winning new customers with customer retention or loyalty.

Although relationship marketing originates from traditional marketing, relationship marketing differs from traditional marketing in that it has dimensions which alter the company's view of traditional marketing (GORDON, 2002).

According to Gordon (2002), the dimensions are: developing new values for customers and sharing this value among them; recognizing the role of each buyer to establish value with the customer and not for the customer; getting the company to plan and align its business processes, its communications, its technology and its staff to maintain the value that each customer wants; maintaining cooperation between the consumer and the seller in real time;

recognizing the customer throughout their consumption life period; building a relationship chain in the company to create the value desired by customers.

Good customer relations are essential for the company. By identifying current customers and maintaining close relationships with them, it is possible to focus attention on the best buyers (BOGMANN, 2000).

To facilitate the company's relationship with customers, Gordon (2002) highlights the use of information technology. According to the author, technology has enabled three elements to serve and manage the individual customer: manufacturing technology, knowledge about the customer and access to the customer.

Manufacturing technology has allowed for mass customization to enable personalized products to be delivered for the same price as a standard product; knowledge about the customer has made it possible to know their needs and desires, while access to the customer has allowed for interesting and enjoyable interaction between customers and the company (GORDON, 2002).

In the view of Peppers and Rogers (2005), companies using relationship marketing need to change their focus from selling to markets and start selling to customers. They must create longer-lasting relationships and use information technology. The strategy would be *one-to-one marketing, the same as Customer Relationship Management.*

Customer Relationship Management (CRM) makes it easier to understand consumer behavior. CRM formulates forecasts and stores the desires, characteristics and needs of individuals in a database (MONTEIRO, 2003).

According to Monteiro (2003) knowing the customer is fundamental, so you have to dedicate yourself to solving problems with them, finding solutions, producing value, developing interdependent strategies, since if one customer has a problem, it will probably affect the other consumer.

The business environment must also be known. By knowing the customers, the competitors and the regulators of the customer's market, the company will be better able to build values that will constitute a competitive advantage for the customer (MONTEIRO, 2003).

Castro (2014) points out that relationship marketing can help preserve the customer's interest in the product or service that the company provides, going through a complex circuit of adding value that includes the company, customers, employees, investors and suppliers. From this perspective, Gordon (2002) mentions that relationship marketing will involve re-evaluating the marketing mix: product, price, place and promotion. The product will need to be the result of a collaborative process. The price will reflect the customer's choice. The marketplace will take on a strategic positioning for the customer's purchase. Promotion will have to use information and communication technology as a means of communication between the consumer and the supermarket retailer.

In relationship marketing, the company needs to focus on retaining customers, so the employee who works directly with the customer must establish a good relationship with them (GORDON, 2002).

Gordon (2002) points out that the employees who deal constantly with the customer are extremely important to the success of relationship marketing. In this context, companies that adopt this process will need to consider their human resources based on a new perception: aligning their capabilities to the task of meeting the expectations of this 'new' customer.

The next subsection explains some concepts relating to price and perceived value.

2.3 Price and Perceived Value

Economic theory pricing models seek to establish the equilibrium price-quantity pair, which increases buyer satisfaction and company revenue (MESQUITA, 2004).

In perfect competition, there are numerous companies selling similar products and none of them is big enough to influence the market price. In this context, the company participating in this type of competition can sell its product at the price established in the market, but cannot sell above this value. In addition to accepting the market price, these companies have to accept the conditions set by the market, so the price is lower when there is a greater supply of the product and higher when there are few units of the product available (CHURCHILL JR.; PETER, 2012). Mesquita (2004, p. 31_32) complements the authors by citing that:

[...] equilibrium price and quantity will be determined impersonally by the forces of supply and demand. The break-even point for an individual firm occurs when the marginal cost (increase in total cost caused by the last unit produced) equals the marginal revenue (revenue obtained by the last unit sold), in this case equal to the price. The consumer, in turn, maximizes his satisfaction by choosing the consumption basket that guarantees him the greatest possible utility, given his limited monetary income.

In monopolistic competition, there are many sellers of the product, but each seller's product differs in some way from the products of the other sellers. This distinction allows the company "some autonomy in setting prices and production. However, the availability of similar products limits the autonomy of prices and makes the demand curve relatively flat along its relevant range" (CHURCHILL JR.; PETER, 2012, p. 322).

According to Mesquita (2004), the researchers from the *Commody* School pooled their efforts to categorize products, and so three categories of products emerged: convenience goods, emergency goods and consumer goods.

Convenience goods are products you buy every day, which are inexpensive and can be used immediately, for example, food. Emergency goods are products that are indispensable in the event of something unforeseen, for example, the cost of medicines. Consumer goods are those whose importance requires the utmost care and can be canceled or transferred to a later date (MESQUITA, 2004).

Melvyn T. Copeland developed his classification based on the purchasing decision-making process, establishing in his prototype: convenience goods, purchase goods and specialty goods. The procedures used for the classification could identify the effort made by the consumer to approach the company, the effort made to compare brands when making the purchase, as well as the degree of preference for the brand (COBRA; BREZZO, 2010).

Another classification of consumer goods is that developed by the *Aspinwall Classification System*, which in its first prototype presented three types of products (red, orange and yellow), and in its second work extended its classification to five types: substitution rate, gross margin, buyer expectation adjustment, duration of product satisfaction and duration of consumer search behavior (COBRA; BREZZO, 2010).

Mesquita (2004) states that price will not always be the most important factor in the consumer's perception, so it is also important to analyze how the consumer understands the value of the product and the price being charged for the goods. In this sense, Nagle and Holden (2003) conceptualize value as the satisfaction that the consumer receives from acquiring a certain product.

In order to determine economic value, Nagle and Holden (2003) claim that some variables must be measured such as: performance, credibility, presentation, maintenance costs, reliability, installation costs and speed of service.

Other variables also influence the buyer's decision: perceived substitute effect, transfer cost, price-quality, expenditure effect, benefit effect, fair price effect and frame effect. These factors produce the buyer's price sensitivity (MESQUITA, 2004).

Price is closely related to economic value, but it plays a more complex role. Kotler and Armstrong (2015) describe price as the amount of money charged for a given service or product. Price is the only element of the marketing mix that generates revenue, unlike the others, which represent costs.

The objectives of pricing are to support efforts to position the product in the market; achieve the desired level of sales; obtain the projected level of profits; compete in terms of market share; provide continuity for the organization and achieve a standard of social responsibility (CHURCHILL JR.; PETER, 2012).

Determining the price is not easy, which is why Kotler and Armstrong (2015) proposed three important pricing strategies: pricing based on customer value, pricing based on costs and pricing based on competition.

Hermes, Cruz and Santini (2016) point out that price perception has an impact on buyer satisfaction and can compromise sales and buyer loyalty. From this perspective, Mesquita (2004) explains that according to economic theory, some buyers seek to satisfy their needs by looking for products with lower prices. Sheth, Mittal and Newman (2001) add that customers make their purchases based on their needs and desires and then try to satisfy them.

Sheth, Mittal and Newman (2001) conceptualize customers as individuals or organizations that play a role in the purchasing transaction. Therefore, in the purchasing process they are essential and play roles such as: buyer, payer and user.

In the next subsection, some concepts relating to the retail segment are described.

2.4 Retail segment

Mesquita (2004) highlights the retail trade as a choice for routine shopping.

A retailer is "an intermediary who is mainly dedicated to selling to end consumers. After purchasing merchandise from manufacturers or wholesalers, retailers engage in individual sales, whether or not they operate stores" (CHURCHILL JR.; PETER, 2012, p. 425).

Parente (2000) cites retail as the activities that involve the process of selling products and services to meet the needs and desires of end consumers. Retailers can be classified as independent, chains, franchises, vertical marketing systems, among others.

Independent retailers are small retailers, most of whom have just one store. Chain retailers are characterized by working with more than one establishment under a single management. Franchises are individually owned and managed establishments that are linked to a large retail chain. Vertical marketing systems are structures in which the members of the channel (producer, wholesaler and retailer) work as an integrated system, seeking to increase the results of the entire channel (PARENTE, 2000).

Retail sales take place through stores or without a store, the latter covering catalog sales, door-to-door sales, internet sales, direct mail, electronic catalogs, among others. Some companies combine the two types of intervention to make it easier for consumers to make their purchases (CHURCHILL JR.; PETER, 2012).

Retail stores come in a variety of formats, with their own characteristics regarding: product lines, location, area, assortment, type of service, among others (BRITO, 1998).

According to the Brazilian Association of Supermarkets - ABRAS (2017b), in June 2017 retail sales in Brazil increased by 1.2% and nominal revenue by 0.8%, both compared to May (series free of seasonal influences).

The segments that contributed the most were textiles, clothing and footwear (5.4%); books, newspapers, magazines and stationery (4.5%); other personal and household articles (2.7%); furniture and household appliances (2.2%); pharmaceutical, medical, orthopaedic, perfumery and cosmetic articles (1.5%); and fuels and lubricants (1.2%) (ABRAS, 2017b).

However, the sectors that contributed the least were hypermarkets, supermarkets, food products, beverages and tobacco, with a fall of 0.4%, followed by office equipment and supplies, IT and communications, with a fall of 2.6% (ABRAS, 2017b).

In June 2016, retail sales grew by 3%. The main highlights were furniture and household appliances (12.7%); textiles, clothing and footwear (4.6%); other personal and household articles (4.3%); pharmaceutical, medical, orthopedic and perfumery articles (3.0%); books, newspapers, magazines and stationery (1.2%) (ABRAS, 2017b).

On the other hand, the sectors that stood out the least were hypermarkets, supermarkets, food products, beverages and tobacco, with 0.8%, and fuels and lubricants, with 0.5% (ABRAS, 2017b).

In June 2017, the expanded retail trade posted a 2.5% increase in sales volume. The segment with the biggest contribution was vehicles and motorcycles, parts and pieces, with 3.8%. However, the sector with the lowest contribution was construction materials, with 1.0% (ABRAS, 2017b).

Compared to the same month a year earlier, the expanded retail sector recorded a 4.4% change in sales volume. The biggest contributor was construction materials, with 7.0%. However, the smallest contribution came from vehicles and motorcycles, parts and pieces, with 3.5% (ABRAS, 2017b).

The data mentioned for the retail trade is shown in Table 1.

Table 1 - Sales volume indicators for retail trade and expanded retail trade

ACTIVITIES	MONTH/PREVIOUS MONTH			previous year's month/year		
	Rate of Change (%)			Rate of Change (%)		
	APRIL	MAY	JUNE	APRIL	MAY	JUNE
RETAIL trade	1,1	0,2	1,2	1,7	2,6	3,0
1. Fuels and lubricants.	-0,7	1,1	1,2	-4,2	-0,4	0,5
2. hypermarkets, supermarkets, food, beverages and tobacco products.	1,3	1,1	-0,4	3,0	0,0	0,8
2.1 Supermarkets and hypermarkets.	2,3	0,6	-0,1	3,5	0,1	2,1
3. Fabrics, clothing and footwear.	4,1	-8,5	5,4	10,8	5,1	4,6
4. Furniture and appliances.	-1,6	1,9	2,2	-0,1	14,0	12,7
4.1 Furniture.	-	-	-	-5,0	2,1	-0,4
4.2 Household appliances.	-	-	-	0,1	17,3	16,9
5. Pharmaceutical , medical articles , orthopedic and perfumery products.	-0,2	0,8	1,5	-2,9	3,5	3,0
6. Books, newspapers, magazines and stationery.	-4,6	-5,0	4,5	-3,4	-0,8	1,2
7. Office, IT and communications equipment and supplies.	8,7	0,0	-2,6	4,4	12,9	5,1
8. Other personal and household articles.	0,5	0,4	2,7	3,4	3,0	4,3
expanded retail trade	1,4	-0,2	2,5	-0,5	4,9	4,4
9. Vehicles and motorcycles, parts and pieces.	-0,3	2,0	3,8	-12,1	5,5	3,5
10. Building materials.	-1,6	2,1	1,0	-1,4	9,5	7,0

Source: ABRAS, 2017b, p.05.

Like Table 1, Graph 1 also shows the volume of retail trade sales in June 2017, highlighting the branches of activity: textiles, clothing and footwear; books, newspapers, magazines and stationery; other articles for personal and household use; furniture and household appliances; pharmaceutical, medical, orthopaedic, perfumery and cosmetic articles; fuels and lubricants; hypermarkets, supermarkets, food products, beverages and tobacco; and office, IT and communications equipment and supplies.

Graph 1 - Retail trade sales volume indicators by sector

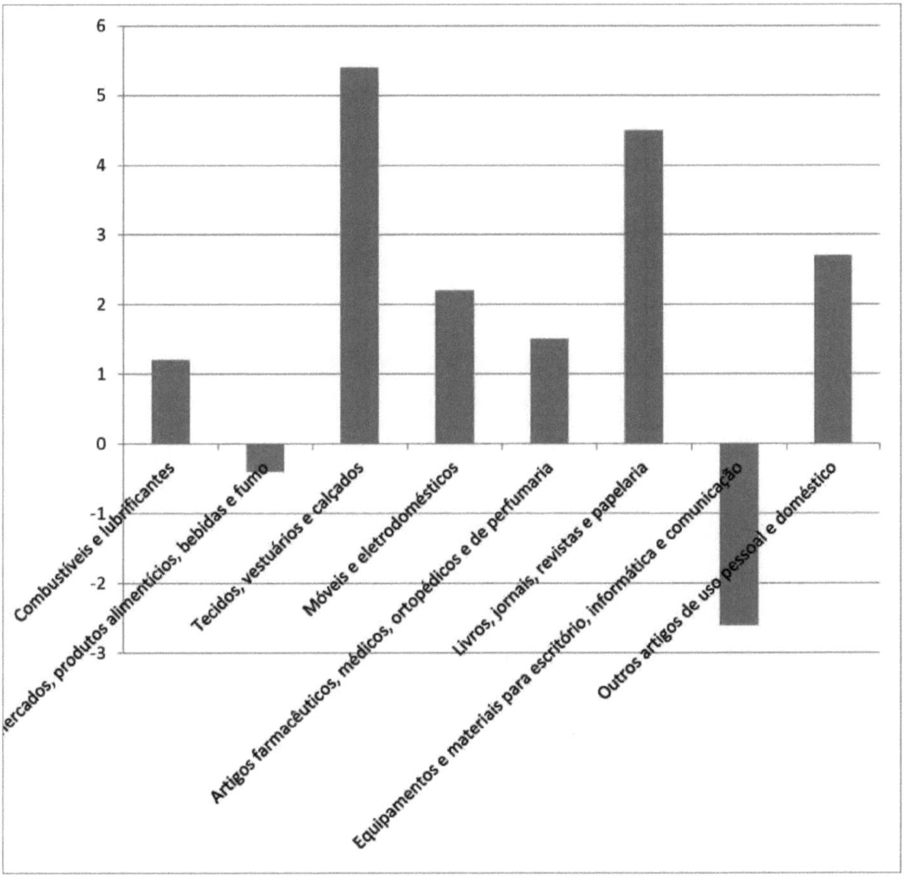

Source: Author, 2017.

According to Mesquita (2004), just like retail, it is also important to understand consumer behavior. To do this, you need to identify issues such as who they are, what they buy, why they buy it, how they go about buying it and the reasons for their satisfaction.

In order to understand consumers, we must distinguish between the roles they play in purchasing transactions: buyer, user and payer (SHETH; MITTAL; NEWMAN, 2001).

For Sheth, Mittal and Newman (2001), the buyer is the individual who carries out the transaction and is responsible for the search. The user refers to the person who will consume the benefits of the product. The payer is the person responsible for paying for the product.

Sheth, Mittal and Newman (2001) point out that consumers can be classified as commercial and domestic.

Commercial consumers are organizations that buy products from other companies. These products are either for consumption or for resale. For example, a building materials store that buys cement can resell it to other companies that work with the same product (LARENTIS, 2009).

Domestic consumers are referred to as household customers. They are the final consumers, the individuals who buy products or services for use or consumption (LARENTIS, 2009).

Há also differentiates between a customer who buys and uses products and one who buys and consumes services. You can have commercial customers who buy products or services and you can have domestic customers who buy products or hire some kind of service (LARENTIS, 2009).

In domestic consumer purchases, there are other roles besides buyer, user and payer. Engel, Blackwell and Miniard (2000) highlight five roles: initiator, influencer, decision-maker, buyer and user.

The initiator is the consumer who is thinking about purchasing a product or service and is looking for information to help them make their decision, for example, a certain person identifies the need to buy a computer and seeks information about the product before purchasing it (ENGEL; BLACKWELL; MINIARD, 2000).

Influencers are consumers whose opinions are important for the evaluation criteria used in decision-making, for example, the opinion of a computer technician for a person who needs to buy a computer (ENGEL; BLACKWELL; MINIARD, 2000).

The decision-maker is the individual who has the authority to decide how to allocate the family's money (ENGEL; BLACKWELL; MINIARD, 2000).

The buyer is the person who makes the purchase, visiting the store, contacting the suppliers, making the payment and taking the product home (ENGEL; BLACKWELL; MINIARD, 2000).

The user is the person responsible for using the product or service purchased (ENGEL; BLACKWELL; MINIARD, 2000).

Mesquita (2004) points out that consumer identification can also be carried out through market segmentation or methods that seek to aggregate groups of consumers with homogeneous behaviors.

As for the products that consumers buy, Mesquita (2004) explains that they are classified by availability or durability.

In terms of availability, there are convenience goods, shopping goods and specialty goods. Convenience goods are low-priced and frequently purchased goods. Shopping goods are those that consumers compare in terms of price, quality and so on. Specialty goods are differentiated, sophisticated products, but which do not give rise to comparisons on the part of the consumer (MESQUITA, 2004).

In terms of durability, Mesquita (2004) classifies goods as durable, non-durable and semi-durable.

Durable goods are those that are used for a longer period of time. Non-durable goods are those whose usefulness ends with consumption. Semi-durable goods have intermediate characteristics between durable and non-durable goods (WOILLER; MATHIAS, 1996).

Why and how people buy are aspects of human behavior, but they are complex and influenced by consumer behavior factors (MESQUITA, 2004).

Satisfaction can be measured by the helpfulness of the sales team, the politeness of the sales staff, how easy it is to find the products, the cleanliness of the store, the assortment, the quality of the products, the quality of the services provided, among others (MESQUITA, 2004).

Mesquita (2004) argues that for pricing the company needs to: define its objectives and analyze the internal and external factors that influence the price. It must also pay attention to environmental variables related to competitors, inflation and legal issues.

For Parente (2000), communication between the retail trade and the consumer to provide information about the store and the store's products is established through advertising, publicity and sales promotion.

Advertising is a process that includes image and information. Through advertising it is possible to obtain details about the products, prices, location and opening hours of the establishment, thus influencing the decision making of the final consumer (HERMES; CRUZ; SANTINI, 2016).

Advertising refers to indirect and impersonal communication through free media. Advertising has the advantage of not costing anything, providing high credibility and reaching a large number of buyers (CHURCHILL JR.; PETER, 2002).

Promotion is marketing pressure exerted in the media and outside it, for a fixed and limited time, aimed at the consumer, retailer or wholesaler, to encourage experiences with a product, increase consumer demand or improve product availability. Promotions usually capture the consumer's attention in order to increase store traffic and impulse purchases (CHURCHILL JR.; PETER, 2002).

Silveira, Campos and Marcon (2006) point out that sales promotions are fundamental marketing tools. According to Mondo and Costa (2013), promotions can be classified as: coupons, special offers, promotional packages, gifts or prizes, competitions or draws and free samples.

Coupons are promotional mechanisms that provide discounts to the buyer at the time of purchase (MONDO; COSTA, 2013).

Special offers are incentives for consumers to visit and buy from the store (CHURCHILL JR.; PETER, 2012). Mondo and Costa (2013) add that the main objective of offers is to influence immediate purchase.

Promotional packages, discounts and sales are special offers that usually encourage the consumer to change brands or try out a new brand. There are also limited-time offers, such as 'pay one and get two' and bonus packs containing extra quantity in the product packaging, such as '40g more cookie', which make the purchase more attractive to the customer (CHURCHILL JR.; PETER, 2012).

Giveaways or prizes are sales promotion procedures that provide the buyer with free merchandise or a lower price when purchasing a service or product (TOLETO; VAZ, 2008).

Contests or sweepstakes are techniques that provide buyers with the opportunity to win trips, real estate, money or any other type of product (MONDO; COSTA, 2013).

Samples are small quantities of products distributed to consumers to induce them to try them out and, consequently, to buy them. The sample can be attached to merchandise, sent by post or even distributed in the retail trade (TOLETO; VAZ, 2008).

Sales promotions usually provide quick sales, most of the time much quicker than advertisements. As such, these types of promotions are considered to be one of the most widely used means of attracting customers to establishments (CHURCHILL JR.; PETER, 2012).

Retailers must pay attention to customer service. Parente (2000) reports that the services provided must be equivalent to the retail strategy, such as: store format, prices, product range and promotional strategies.

According to Mesquita (2004), the store is the interface between the buyer and the retailer, at which point the consumer shows his buying behavior and his level of satisfaction or even dissatisfaction.

Mesquita (2004) explains that decisions about the store should be the main factor in developing the retailer's image, as well as increasing sales. From this perspective, decisions cover external and internal presentation, *layout and* the way products are displayed in the retail environment.

Deciding on a retail location is fundamental and is fraught with difficulties. Therefore, Parente (2000) mentions that in addition to the arguments set out above, the location must also be analyzed very carefully, seeking to assess existing and potential demand, target audience, competitors, among other important aspects.

3 ENVIRONMENT

The first plans for supermarket retailing emerged in 1920 in the United States, but it wasn't until 1934 that the term supermarket came to be widely accepted by people who, directly or indirectly, came into contact with these retail stores (STILMAN, 1962).

Stilman (1962) mentions that the supermarket only spread throughout the world after the Second World War.

In Brazil, the first supermarket experiences began in 1947. In 1947, Frigorifico Wilson appeared in Sao Paulo, selling groceries through self-service and meat in a closed refrigerated counter with personal service. In 1949, another establishment appeared in Sao Paulo, Depósito Popular, which sold food in a self-service system (VAROTO, 2006).

According to Varoto (2006), Frigorifico Wilson and Depòsito popular were unsuccessful, but they helped lay the foundations for the new retail model in the country. From this perspective, Ferreira (2013) reports that the first Brazilian supermarket was Supermercado Sirva-se S.A, founded in 1953 in the city of Sao Paulo and owned by Souza Cruz.

Ferreira (2013) points out that Supermercado Sirva-se offered a new concept in food sales for Brazilians, who were timidly coming into contact with the modernity brought about by television.

Supermercados Sirva-se S.A. was the first to use a layout and equipment similar to those in the United States. With 800 square meters of sales area, it had the characteristics of modern supermarkets, such as divisions by sections, spaces for product advertisements and the use of the ends of gondolas to promote products. It was the first to sell meat, fruit and vegetables in the same place, as well as a grocery range (VAROTO, 2006, p. 89).

Other supermarkets sprang up from the Sirva Supermarket, with the Peg-Pag Supermarket standing out in 1954, which became the standard for supermarkets in terms of store layout, customer service and employee training (VAROTO, 2006).

In the following years, several supermarket retail stores opened in the country, but it wasn't until the early 1970s that the first hypermarkets appeared, occupying areas of three thousand square meters, with restaurants and snack bars, offering ample parking, selling food, household appliances, clothes, gift items and a wide variety of products. Examples of hypermarkets include Makro, which opened in 1973, and Carrefour, which opened in São Paulo in 1975 (VAROTO, 2006).

Ferreira (2013) argues that in 1990, many changes impacted the retail sector, such as the opening up of trade and, consequently, increased internal competition.

The entry of international retail chains, such as Walmart (USA), Casino (France), Sonae (Portugal), Jerônimo Martins (Portugal) and Ahold (Holland), which were facing saturation in their home markets and were looking for growth and profitability opportunities in emerging countries, and the internalization of more modern concepts of operations imposed the need for profound transformations on the part of Brazilian companies (FERREIRA, 2013, p. 74_75).

A survey carried out by the Economics and Research Department of the Brazilian Supermarket Association - ABRAS, in partnership with Nielsen Consulting, highlighted that the Brazilian supermarket sector exceeded 89,000 establishments in 2016, which means an increase of 0.5% over 2015, when the number of stores in the sector reached 88,600 (ABRAS, 2017a).

In addition, according to the survey, there was an increase in the number of *checkouts*, from 222,800 in 2015 to 225,000 in 2016 (ABRAS, 2017a).

In July 2017, ABRAS (2017b) reported that real self-service sales increased by 4.21% and nominal variation of 4.46% compared to June of that year, as shown in Table 2.

The Association's president, Joâo Sanzovo Neto, pointed out that supermarket retail sales have been showing moderate growth in 2017 (ABRAS, 2017b).

Table 2 - Nominal and real changes in self-service

Variations Analysis period 07/2017	Nominal Variation	Real Change (IPCA/IBGE)
July/2017 x June/2017	4,46%	4,21%
July/2017 x June/2016	2,22%	-0,50%
Cumulative/year	4,80%	0,73%

Source: ABRAS, 2017b, p.01.

The consumer behavior research company GFK, in partnership with the Brazilian Supermarket Association, found that confidence in the Brazilian supermarket segment had improved from 46% in June to 64% in August 2017 (ABRAS, 2017d).

According to research by GFK and ABRAS, the expectation for supermarket retail should continue to rise gradually, which should lead to new investments in the supermarket segment (ABRAS, 2017c).

In addition, the study by GFK and ABRAS found that changes in consumer behavior are becoming influential factors for the future of the supermarket sector. Currently, consumers are concerned about the environmental impact of what they are consuming. As a result, supermarket retailers are paying more attention to their environmental responsibilities, labels, ingredients and healthiness (ABRAS 2017c).

In the municipality of Palmas, capital of the state of Tocantins, the first supermarkets to set up shop were Rede Caçulinha Supermarket, founded in 1999 (EMPRESAS, 1999) and Quartetto Supermercado, opened in 1999 (QUARTETTO, 2017).

Supermercado Caçulinha's main activity was retailing in general, with a predominance of food products. The supermarket closed down in 2010 (EMPRESAS, 1999).

Quartetto Supermercado operates in supermarket retail, with a predominance of food products. Quartetto Supermarket focuses on a pleasant environment, quality, variety of products, excellent service and fair prices (QUARTETTO, 2017).

In addition to these, other supermarkets stand out in the city of Palmas for their importance, quality and variety of products, such as the Big Supermarket, with its first store installed in 2007 (BIG, 2015); Atacadao Wholesaler, belonging to the Carrefour Group, opened in 2009 (CONEXÂO, 2015); Makro Wholesaler, opened in 2009 (CONEXÂO, 2009); Extra Hypermarket, belonging to the Pao de Açùcar Group, opened in 2010 (EXAME, 2010).

Parente (2000) distinguishes between types of supermarket, classifying them as superstores, conventional supermarkets, compact supermarkets and hypermarkets.

Superstores have around thirty *checkouts* and 400 m^2 and sell food, electronics and more. Conventional supermarkets are medium-sized stores and deal in food. Compact supermarkets have an average of two to six *checkouts.* Hypermarkets are stores that have up to 10,000m^2 and sell approximately fifty thousand items of products, with an emphasis on food, non-food products, among others (PARENTE 2000).

According to Lepsch (1996), sales in the retail segment are not predominantly physical, but also involve services. (2013) explain that services are used to describe the tasks carried out by salespeople and others who accompany the sale of a product, and who help them to exchange or use it.

Services have several unique characteristics that almost always have a significant impact on the development of a marketing program. These special characteristics can cause specific problems, and almost always result in marketing mix decisions that are substantially different from those encountered in connection with product marketing. Some of these most important characteristics are intangibility, inseparability, perishability and fluctuating demand, customer relationship, consumer effort, and uniformity (PETER; DONNELLY JR., 2013, p. 233).

Lepsch (1996) lists as services and service attributes the mix of prices and products offered; the store environment; its image; courtesy service; parking; *layout;* credit card; among others.

Parente (2000) points out that retail activities can also be carried out over the *internet*, by telephone, as well as in the consumer's home and not just in a physical environment.

According to Engel, Blackwell and Miniard (2000), the image of the retail segment is measured by dimensions, which result in variables. However, these variables are divided into the following categories: a) location; b) nature and quality of variety or assortment; c) price; d) advertising and promotion; e) sales staff; f) services provided; g) physical attributes of the establishment; h) nature of the store's customers; i) store atmosphere; and j) service and post-transaction satisfaction.

Kotler and Keller (2006) define location, plaza (or distribution channel) as the place where goods are available for consumption or use by end consumers.

Location is an essential variable for retail. Some elements of a good location assessment include: store size, parking capacity, access to public transportation, visibility, pedestrian flow, among others (ENGEL; BLACKWELL; MINIARD, 2000).

The breadth and quality of assortments are determining factors in the final consumer's choice of store (ENGEL; BLACKWELL; MINIARD, 2000). (2013) classify quality as the degree of excellence or superiority that a product possesses.

The importance of price in deciding which store to buy varies according to the type of product. Price has become an important variable when choosing a supermarket, given the competition and the poor level of service. However, the importance of price depends on the nature of the consumer, since there are customers who value other attributes, such as convenience, and may pay more in exchange for what they prioritize (ENGEL; BLACKWELL; MINIARD, 2000).

Many consumers have access to a variety of media tools via *smartphones* and *tablets*, which give them instant access to blogs and information content, and they can use apps to find the lowest prices or find out what their friends are buying, making it easier to find alternative options and making them more price-sensitive (BOTELHO; GUISSONI, 2016, p. 597).

Advertising provides information about the store and the prices of products or services. Promotion, on the other hand, enables the consumer, retailer or wholesaler to encourage experiences with a product, increase buyer demand and also improve the availability of merchandise (CHURCHILL JR.; PETER, 2012).

According to Mondo and Costa (2013), sales promotion is considered one of the most important marketing actions, especially when it comes to attracting consumers.

In the retail sector, confidence in retail salespeople is usually low, as training with sales staff and relationships with consumers are often lacking. In this context, retailers are being pressured by consumers to rethink their business and deliver to the customer what they expect from services, as well as sales assistance (ENGEL; BLACKWELL; MINIARD, 2000).

With regard to the provision of services, Engel, Blackwell and Miniard (2000) point out that services such as the exchange of goods, customer delivery and credit services affect the image of the establishment. The authors give the example of supermarkets that provide qualified staff to reduce the time consumers have to wait in line.

The services offered to buyers are essential factors in differentiating the establishment from other competitors, thus helping to satisfy end consumers (HERMES; CRUZ; SANTINI, 2016).

The physical attributes of the store, such as air conditioning, toilets, lighting, *layout,* architecture, among others, are internal and external image factors that are decisive in the choice of shopping location (ENGEL; BLACKWELL; MINIARD, 2000).

Hermes, Cruz and Santini (2016) state that the external retail environment, such as architecture, store windows, signs and the store entrance, are important factors, as these elements attract the target audience to the store.

According to Engel, Blackwell and Miniard (2000), the type of shopper who makes a purchase in an establishment can affect the choice of other consumers due to the propagated willingness to combine self-image with the image of the store.

The store's atmosphere is a factor that has certain effects on consumers and can help them to purchase a product that might otherwise go unnoticed (HERMES; CRUZ; SANTINI, 2016).

Consumers are looking for service and after-sales satisfaction, especially when it comes to sales of furniture, household appliances and cars. Therefore, valuing services is fundamental in the retail trade (ENGEL; BLACKWELL; MINIARD, 2000).

4 METHODOLOGY

The following is a description of the research approach and data collection technique.

4.1 Research Approach

This project will use a qualitative approach. According to Santos and Candeloro (2006), qualitative research provides a survey of subjective data based on the testimonies of the people interviewed, i.e. the search for information relevant to the universe to be analyzed.

Qualitative research does not seek to estimate variables, but rather to qualitatively study, in an inductive way, the data collected through data collection techniques. These techniques include, for example, interviews, case studies, questionnaires, systematic observation, among others (SANTOS; CANDELORO, 2006).

4.2 Data Collection Technique

Interviews will be used to collect data. Marconi and Lakatos (2003) conceptualize an interview as a conversation between two individuals, in order for one of them to acquire information on a particular subject, by means of a conversation of a professional nature.

The interview will be semi-structured. According to Marconi and Lakatos (2003), in a semi-structured interview the questions are open-ended and can be answered through informal conversation.

The interview will be conducted with thirteen clients/consumers in various locations in the municipality of Palmas, Tocantins. For this purpose, a simple random survey will be used. Gil (2002) mentions that the simple random technique consists of randomly selecting the people to be interviewed.

The basic questionnaire for the interview can be found in Appendix A - Questionnaire.

In order to facilitate understanding and later transcription of the data, a tape recorder will be used during the interviews.

5 PRESENTATION AND ANALYSIS OF DATA

This section aims to show the results of the research. To facilitate data analysis, the interviewees have been given the pseudonyms: E1, E2, E3, E4, E5, E6, E7, E8, E9, E10, E11, E12, E13.

5.1 Profile of the interviewees

Based on the qualitative approach, the profile of the interviewees is shown in Table 1 and Graphs 2, 3 and 4.

Table 1 - Profile of interviewees

Interviewee	Age	Sex	Profession
E1	50	Female	Public Servants
E2	24	Female	Civil engineer
E3	21	Female	Administrative Assistant
E4	29	Female	Finance Manager
E5	26	Female	Journalist
E6	18	Male	Graphic Designer
E7	42	Male	Administrator
E8	45	Female	Domestic
E9	33	Female	Physiotherapist
E10	26	Female	Clerk
E11	37	Male	Journalist
E12	48	Male	Building Technician
E13	46	Female	Housewife

Source: Prepared by the author, 2018.

Graph 2 - Age

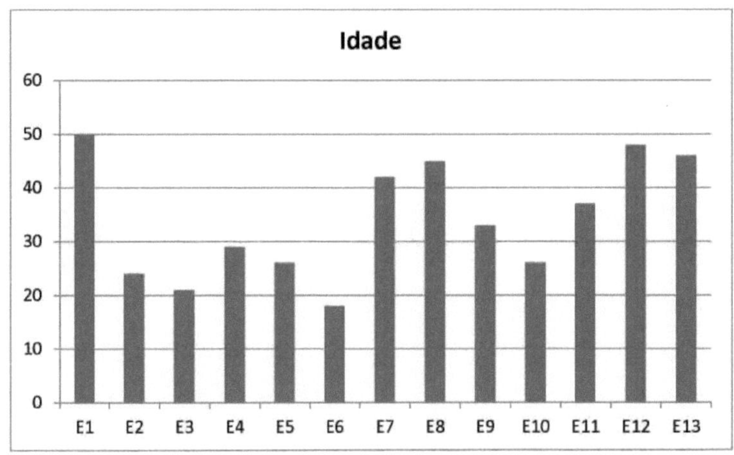

Source: Prepared by the author, 2018.

Graph 3 - Sex

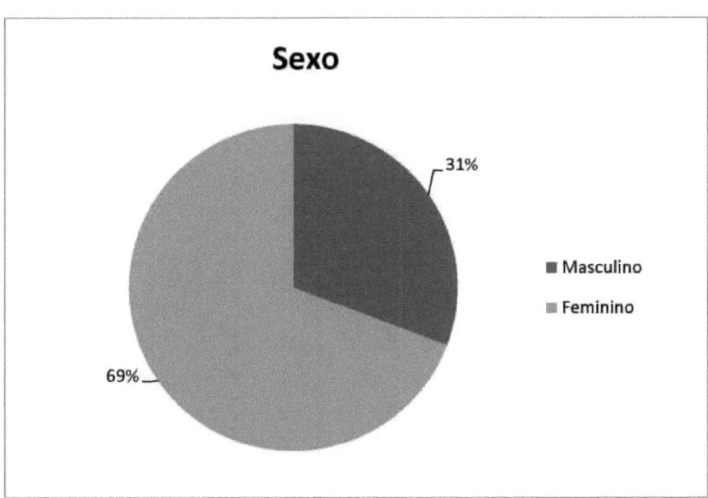

Source: Prepared by the author, 2018.

Graph 4 - Profession

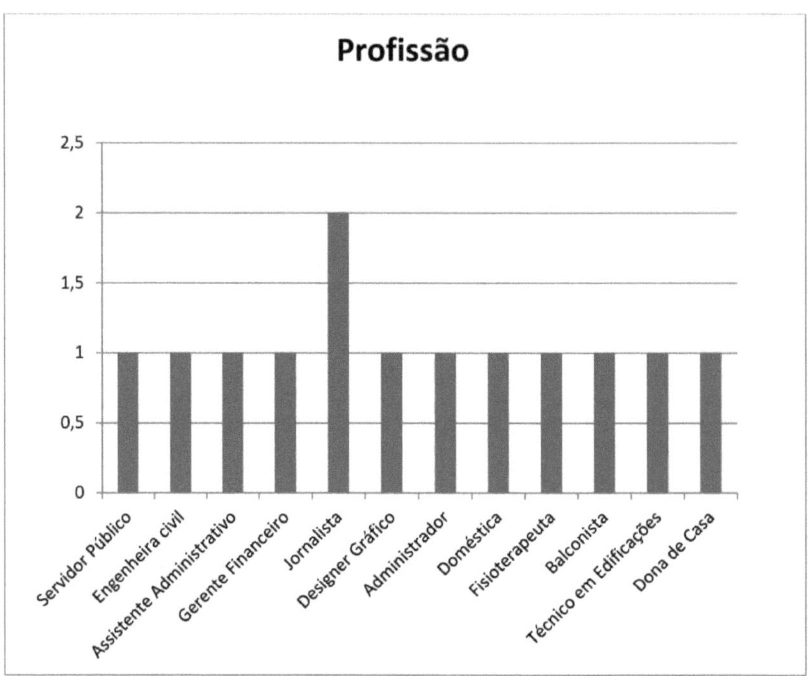

5.2 Analysis of results

5.2.1 Square

The square/location has a great influence on the flow of clients/consumers. This can be seen in the statements made by E3 and E4: "Yes, because there's the question of making the purchase and taking it away, so location is very important" (E3). "Yes, location is important, right? That it's close to home" (E4).

When asked if the supermarket was close to their home or work. Ten of the respondents reported buying from supermarkets close to their home, two mentioned close to work and one said that it suited their situation. Parente and Kato (2001) add that supermarket retail sales are normally made by customers who live close to the establishment where they shop.

Location is fundamental, but it doesn't always become decisive, as E6 and E12 demonstrate:

Not always. Sometimes when there's a promotion it's more advantageous for me to go to one that's a bit further away than to one that's closer, almost always the smaller supermarkets, which are always the ones closest to the more central areas, are more... more expensive than the hypermarkets (E6).

Not always. It's also based on other factors: product quality, options, variety (E12).

According to Kotler and Keller (2006), consumers need differentiated services. From this perspective, parking becomes an essential attribute in supermarket retail, as E2, E5 and E12 state. "Absolutely. Because you have somewhere to leave your car, right?" (E2). "It's very important because it makes it easier, there's somewhere to leave my vehicle safely and not in the middle of the street where something could happen to it" (E5). "Yes, it's certainly important, even with the size of the city today, parking in a supermarket is very important" (E12).

5.2.2 Internal layout of the supermarket

Eight people reported that it was easy to find the products they needed on the shelves of the supermarkets where they shop. I could see this in what E4 and E11 said. "Yes, it's easy" (E4). "Yes, because the general layout of the supermarket and the distribution of the products are similar, right? The internal communication is easy to access, the communication indicating the products, the product sections are easy" (E11). In this context, it can be said that most of the supermarkets mentioned in the survey have a good internal layout when it comes to the products on the shelves.

With regard to specific products, the people questioned had already needed help to locate a product on the shelves. E9 explains that: "[...] especially the products I need in relation to lactose, I always look for in the supermarket because I can't find it easily, it's not always on the labels."

Parente (2000) points out that retailers should provide a store format that makes it easier to locate products, as well as having specific product lines.

As for queues, only one of the interviewees said he didn't have to queue when paying for his purchases. The others said they were constantly queuing and added: "[...] there would have to be more cashiers" (E3). "What I notice here in Palmas is that they've mainly taken away the people who pack, so the person who buys is the person who packs their purchase and this takes up more time and leads to longer queues" (E9).

E12 adds that "there's no feeling on the part of the administrator. It's about realizing that this is a peak time and that there's a need to increase the number of cashiers".

Queues at checkouts are a negative factor for supermarkets and in turn cause consumer dissatisfaction.

5.2.3 Products

Seven of the consumers described finding the products they needed easily in the supermarket. This was explained by E4 and E6: "Yes" (E4). "When it comes to food, always" (E6).

The other informants said they 'couldn't' or 'didn't always' find the products they needed in the supermarket:

No. I believe that due to the economic climate, sometimes a supermarket is conditioned to buy products that will make a financial return and not the adversity of serving the customer who is looking for them (E12).

Not always. In my case, there are certain things I can't find, so I end up going to another supermarket to supplement what I need (E9).

The lack of products on the shelves is a negative factor and shows that these retailers are not adequately developing customer relationship marketing.

When asked about brands, eight people mentioned not finding their favorite brands in the supermarket where they shop. Kotler and Armstrong (2015) add that consumers see brands as an important part of the product and develop a long-lasting relationship with them, and establishments that stop supplying certain brands tend to lose customers or leave them dissatisfied, as shown by E5 and E12:

Yes, I would stop buying there. Because it wouldn't really meet what I wanted, so I think so (E5).

This happens a lot, that I don't find the product I want to consume and I have to make a real pilgrimage there to attract the product I want, right? And sometimes my fuel consumption increases because I go looking for it, but I don't buy it there because I want to consume the product I already know. It may be traditionalism, conservatism, whatever you want to call it, but it's easier to consume a product you know (E12).

As for variety, the participants in the survey were unanimous in stating that the supermarkets they buy from have a variety of products. This was identified by E5 and E12. "The supermarket I go to does. There is some variety. There could be more because they limit themselves to certain products" (E5). There are a lot of products that I don't consume, but there are a lot of other options (E12).

5.2.4 Price

Eleven of the interviewees claimed to compare the prices of the supermarket referenced in the survey with other supermarkets. E4 reflects the consensus of the majority. "Yes, I do". Price research is one of the characteristics of consumer behavior. Lopes and Silva (2011) point out that the Nicosia model establishes that buying behavior is preceded by price research.

Two of the respondents said they didn't compare price, but rather factors such as location and time available. "No, I buy there because it's easier, it's closer to my house, because of the location" (E3). "Not usually, because I also analyze my time and commute" (E11).

Eight people would stop shopping at their usual supermarket because of the high price. I could see this in E1: "Sometimes I do, the price is much higher". The other respondents claimed to continue shopping and E9 added: "You compare the price and what you'll spend on fuel to go to the other supermarket ends up being the same. Sometimes I end up buying more because it's closer, because I won't have to go to another one further away from home".

Mesquita (2004) elucidates that price is not always the most important factor in consumer perception, and this can be seen in what E9 said. In this sense, we must analyze how the consumer understands the value of the product and the price that is included in the merchandise.

As for positive and negative comments about prices in supermarkets, most of the interviewees said they had heard positive comments. "I've heard positive comments that they're cheap in certain sectors" (E5). "I've heard positive comments, saying that they have very good prices, very good prices, very affordable prices" (E6).

5.2.5 Promotion

All the supermarkets mentioned in the survey run promotions. These promotions are advertised on *Instagram*; *WhatsApp*; *Facebook*; car, radio and TV ads; *folders* and in the supermarket. *Internet* advertising is one of the most important forms of media for marketing today.

Eleven people would stop shopping at their usual supermarket if another supermarket started offering better deals. E3 and E4 added: "Yes, but not if it's far from my house. If it's close by and has better quality, I'll go" (E3). "Yes, if there's another supermarket closer to my house and it has promotions, and if it's at a lower price, more affordable than there, but it's certainly advantageous" (E4).

Consumers would like to see the products that make up the basic basket, personal hygiene, meat, vegetables and milk, go on sale. Graph 5 shows this in detail.

Graph 5 - Products that consumers would like to see on sale

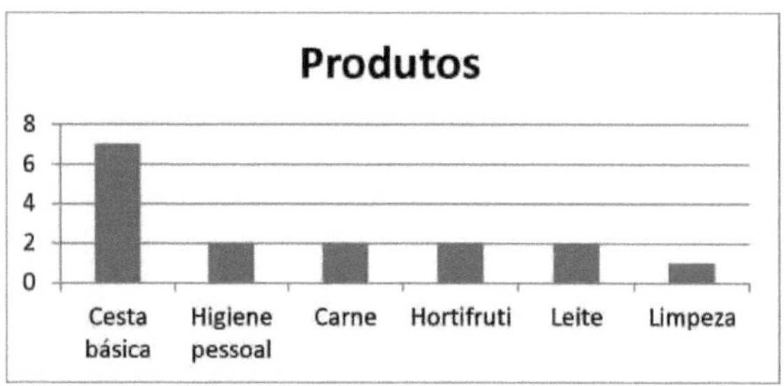

Source: Prepared by the author, 2018.

The most cited products were the items that make up the basic food basket (Graph 5), with rice standing out (Graph 6).

Graph 6 - Products in the food basket

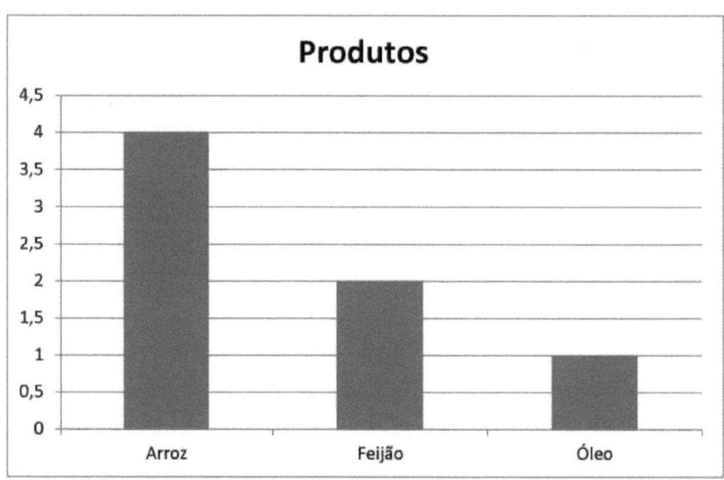

Source: Prepared by the author, 2018.

Ten of the interviewees have been to the supermarket because of a promotion and ended up buying other products. E5, E7 and E8 add: "Sometimes people go to buy just one product that's on sale and end up leaving with a full trolley full of other things that weren't on the list" (E5). "You don't go to a supermarket to buy just one product that's on sale, do you" (E7). "They lure us in with a promotion and we end up taking something else that we weren't even going to buy" (E8).

Promotions usually attract the consumer's attention, increase store traffic and impulse purchases, as Churchill Jr. and Peter (2002) point out.

5.2.6 Service

Ten of the interviewees described being well looked after in the supermarkets where they shop (Graph 7). In this context, it can be said that these retailers value good customer service.

Graph 7 - Customer service

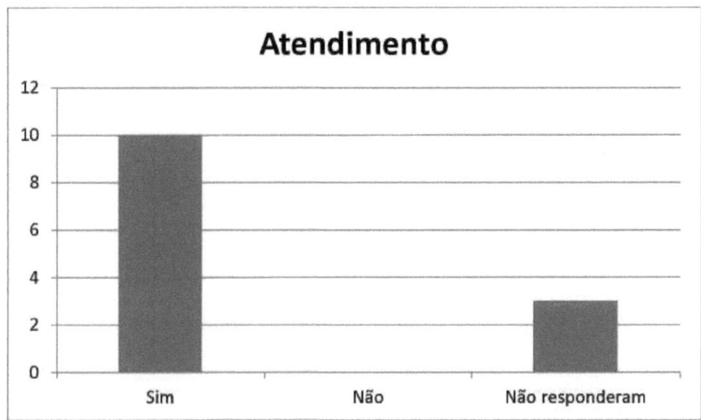

Source: Prepared by the author, 2018.

Employees who constantly deal with the customer are extremely important to the success of relationship marketing and therefore need to be trained to provide good customer service.

5.2.7 General

When choosing a supermarket, respondents described the importance of attributes such as: hygiene of the premises; quality of the product; availability of products; size of the supermarket; parking; location; price; promotion; service and organization. Graph 8 shows this in detail.

Graph 8 - Key attributes for choosing a supermarket

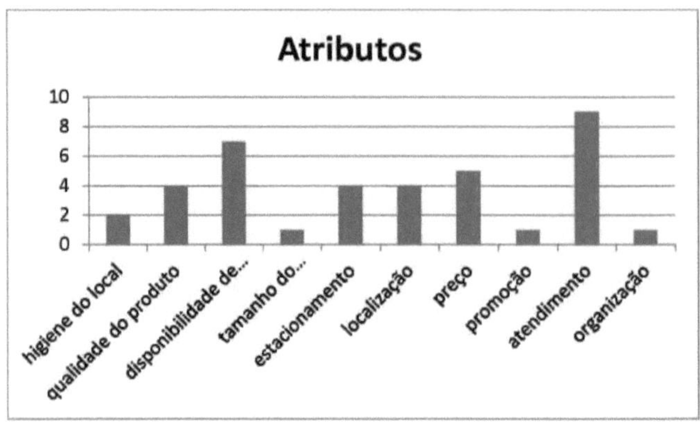

Source: Prepared by the author, 2018.

All the items described in Graph 8 are important when choosing a supermarket, but some are more important, such as customer service, product availability and price.

With regard to what would make them stop shopping at their usual supermarket. The respondents described attributes such as: the lack of hygiene in the store; poor quality products; a lack of product *mix*; expired products; competition; high prices; misleading advertising; poor service and a reduction in the number of *checkouts*. Graph 9 shows the details.

Graph 9 - Determining factors for not shopping in a supermarket

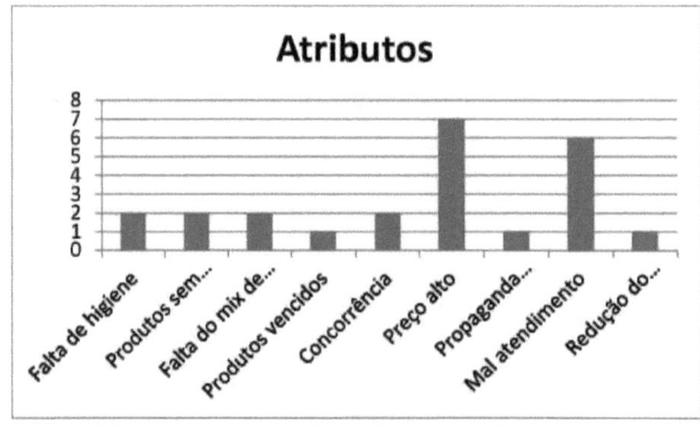

Source: Prepared by the author, 2018.

The items mentioned in Graph 9 would cause consumers to stop shopping at their usual supermarket, but some of them with more emphasis, such as high prices and poor service.

Keeping customers satisfied is essential for supermarket retailers. Therefore, self-service stores need to pay attention to retail strategies such as: knowing their target audience; building customer loyalty; investing in good customer service; using social media to advertise; having adequate prices; product diversity; developing promotional strategies; having a store format; among other services.

CONCLUSION

Based on the answers given by the interviewees, it can be seen that the following items: square, internal layout of the supermarket, product, price, promotion and service are relevant attributes in supermarket retail purchasing decisions.

The square/location has a lot of influence on the flow of customers, as consumers seek to buy products in supermarkets close to their homes.

The internal layout of products is a highly prized item. In this sense, it is essential that retailers provide a store format that makes it easier for customers to locate goods.

The supermarket must have a variety of products. The lack of merchandise on the shelves is a negative factor and proves that retailers are not developing customer relationship marketing correctly.

Price is highly valued by consumers/customers. Lopes and Silva (2011) explain that the consumer behavior model established by Nicosia has as its fundamental characteristic price research on the part of the consumer/customer.

Promotions attract customers to the store and, in turn, impulse purchases. Publicizing promotions online and traditionally is key to increasing sales in the retail sector.

Consumers/customers look for various attributes to repurchase in a supermarket, among them customer service, since a survey carried out in 2017 in the municipality of Palmas, capital of the state of Tocantins, revealed that customer service is the attribute most valued by respondents.

Although service is the attribute most cited in the survey for repurchasing in a supermarket, other attributes are also important, such as the hygiene of the place; the quality of the product; the availability of products; the size of the supermarket; the parking lot; the square; the price; the promotion and the internal layout.

Through the research carried out in Palmas, it was possible to identify that consumers/customers are more demanding and this is causing changes in business strategies, making retailers opt for quality and consumer satisfaction. The supermarkets mentioned in the survey strive for good service, product quality, hygiene, promotions to attract customers, good internal layout and an adequate price. However, some of them do not live up to expectations in terms of the variety of products on their shelves.

For future studies, it is suggested that research be carried out to identify the attributes of repurchase in supermarkets in other Brazilian capitals, allowing the results of this study to be compared with those of other consumers.

REFERENCES

ABRAS (2017a). Available at: <http://www.abrasnet.com.br/economia-e- pesquisa/ranking-abras/os-numeros-do-setor/>. Accessed on: September 12, 2017.

ABRAS (2017b). Available at: <http://www.abras.com.br/economia-e- pesquisa/boletim-de-economia-artigo/>. Accessed on: September 11, 2017.

ABRAS (2017c). Available at: <http://www.abrasnet.com.br/clipping.php?area=20&clipping=62404>. Accessed on: September 11, 2017.

ABRAS (2017d). Available at: <http://www.abrasnet.com.br/clipping.php?area=20&clipping=62414>. Accessed on: September 5, 2017.

BOGMANN, I. M. **Relationship marketing:** loyalty strategies and their financial implications. Sao Paulo: Nobel, 2000.

BOTELHO, D.; GUISSONI, L. **Retail:** competitiveness and innovation. RAI, Sao Paulo, v. 55, n. 6, p.596_599, nov./dez. 2016.

BRITO, D. **What is the right format for your store?** Revista Super-Hiper, Sao Paulo, v. 24, n. 277, p. 74_77, set. 1998.

CASTRO, A. D. P. D; SOUSA, C. V. **Marketing mix strategy in supermarkets:** a study with managers in Entre Rios de Minas/MG. Reavi, v.2, n. 2, p. 87_99, dec. 2013.

CHURCHILL JR. G. A.; PETER, J. P. **Marketing:** creating value for customers. 3ª ed. Sao Paulo: Saraiva, 2012.

COBRA, M.; BREZZO, R. **O novo marketing.** Rio de Janeiro: Elsevier, 2010.

COLLIS, J.; HUSSEY, R. **Research in administration:** a practical guide for undergraduate and postgraduate students. 2. ed. Porto Alegre: Bookman, 2005.

ENGEL, J. F.; BLACKWELL, R. D.; MINIARD, P. W. **Comportamento do consumidor.** Rio de Janeiro: Livros técnicos e cientificos Editora S.A., 2000.

FERREIRA, P. R. D. A. **The process of globalization of mass retailing and competitive struggles:** the case of the supermarket sector in Brazil. 2013. 250f. v.1. Thesis (Luiz Antônio da Rocha Dib) Federal University of Rio de Janeiro, Rio de Janeiro, 2013.

FILHO, D. B. F.; SILVA JR. J. A. **Vision beyond reach:** an introduction to factor analysis. Opiniao Pùblica, Campinas, v.16, n. 1, jun. 2010.

GETÚLIO VARGAS FOUNDATION - FGV. **Sector analysis:** supermarkets. 2011. Available at:

<https://cev.fgv.br/sites/cev.fgv.br/files/Analise%20Setorial_Supermercados_2011.pd   f>. Accessed on: September 10, 2017.

GIL, A. C. **Como elaborar projetos de pesquisa.** 4. ed. - Sâo Paulo: Atlas, 2002.

GORDON, I. **Relationship marketing:** strategies, techniques and technologies to win customers and keep them forever. 5.ed. Sâo Paulo: Futura, 2002.

GRONROOS, C. **Marketing:** management and services. 2. ed. Rio de Janeiro: Campus, 2003.

GOLSTEIN, M.; ALMEIDA, H. S. **Critiques of integrative models of consumer behavior.** Revista de Administraçâo, Sâo Paulo, v.35, n. 1, p.14_22, jan./mar. 2000.

HERMES, L. C. R.; CRUZ, C. M. L; SANTINI, I. **Competitive advantages of the retail mix from a VRIO perspective:** a case study in an independent supermarket. Revista Brasileira de Marketing, Sâo Paulo, v. 15, n. 3, p.737_389, jul./set. 2016.

HONORATO, G. **Knowing marketing.** Barueri - SP: Manole, 2004.

KOTLER, P.; ARMSTRONG, G. **Marketing principles.** 15. ed. Sâo Paulo: Pearson, 2015.

; KELLER, Kevin Lane. **Marketing Management.** 12. ed. Sâo Paulo: Pearson, 2006.

LARENTIS, F. **Consumer Behavior and Relationship Marketing.** Curitiba: IESDE Brasil, 2009.

LOPES, E. L.; SILVA, D. **Integrative models of consumer behavior:** a theoretical review. Revista Brasileira de Marketing, Sâo Paulo, v. 10, n. 3, p.03_23, Sep./Dec. 2011.

LEPSCH, S. L. **Precificação em supermercados:** um estudo exploratório junto a vinte empresas brasileiras.1996. 97 f. (Dissertation) - Department of Administration and Accounting, University of São Paulo, USP, São Paulo, 1996.

MALHOTRA, N. K. **Marketing research:** an applied orientation. 6. ed. Porto Alegre: Bookman, 2012.

MARCONI, M. A.; LAKATOS, E.M. **Fundamentos de metodologia cientifica.** 5. ed. Sâo Paulo: Atlas, 2003.

MESQUITA, J. M. C. D. **Explanatory attributes of repurchase intention in supermarkets.** 2004. 253f. v.1. Thesis (José Edson Lara) Universidade Federal de Minas Gerais, Belo Horizonte, 2004.

MINGOTTI, S. A. **Data analysis using multivariate statistical methods:** an applied approach. Belo Horizonte: UFMG, 2005.

MONDO, T. S.; COSTA, J. L. P. **The influence of sales promotion in attracting customers:** a study in the hotel industry in Santa Catarina. Revista Brasileira de Marketing, Sâo Paulo, v. 12, n. 2, p.87_107, abr./jun. 2013.

MONTEIRO, M. C. W. **Marketing de relacionamento:** proposta de um plano de marketing de relacionamento para a Genyus Baterias. 2003. Dissertation Getúlio Vargas Foundation, Rio de Janeiro, 2003.

NAGLE, T. T.; HOLDEN, R. K. **Pricing strategy and tactics.** São Paulo: Prentice Hall, 2003.

NIELSEN, H. P. **Changes in the Brazilian market:** family is not all the same. 2017. Available at: <http://www.nielsen.com/br/pt/insights/reports/2017/mudancas-no- mercado-brasileiro-familia-nao-e-tudo-igual.html>. Accessed on: August 20, 2017.

PARENTE, J. **Varejo no Brasil:** gestâo e estratégia, Sâo Paulo: Atlas, 2000.

PEPPERS, D; ROGERS, M. **Return on customers:** creating maximum value from your scarcest resource: a revolutionary way to measure and strengthen your business. Rio de Janeiro: Elsevier, 2005.

PETER, J. P.; DONNELLY JR, J. H. **Introduction to marketing:** creating value for customers. São Paulo: Saraiva, 2013.

SANTOS, V.; CANDELORO, R. J. **Trabalhos acadêmicos:** uma orientação para a pesquisa e normas técnicas. Porto Alegre-RS: AGE, 2006.

SCIENTIFIC PERIODICALS ELECTRONIC LIBRARY - SPELL. Available at: <http://www.spell.org.br/>. Accessed on September 10, 2017.

SHETH, J. N.; MITTAL, B.; NEWMAN, B. I. **Customer behavior:** going beyond consumer behavior. Sâo Paulo: Atlas, 2001.

SILVEIRA, R. B.; CAMPOS, L. M; S.; MARCON, R. **Segmentation and promotion in fundraising:** a study in third sector foundations. Revista Faces R. Adm. Belo Horizonte, v. 5, n. 2, p.25_40, mai./ago. 2006.

SLONGO, L. A.; MUSSNICH, R. **Customer service and relationship marketing in the** Porto Alegre **hotel sector**. Revista de Administraçâo Contemporânea, Curitiba, v. 9, n. 1, mar. 2005.

SOLOMON, M. R.. **Consumer behavior:** buying, owning and being. 11ª. ed. Porto Alegre: Bookman, 2016.

STILMAN, M. **The supermarkets of Sao Paulo**. Sao Paulo: USP, 1962.

STONE, M.; WOODCOCK, N. **Relationship marketing**. Sao Paulo: Littera Mundi, 1998.

WHOLESALE SUPERMARKET. 2015. Available at: <http://conexaoto.com.br/2015/08/14/atacadao-abre-novo-centro-de-distribuicao-em-palmas-com-250-empregos-direct-e-indiretos>. Accessed on: September 1, 2017.

SUPERMERCADO BIG. 2015. Available at: <http://www.superbig.com.br/institucional/>. Accessed on: September 3, 2017.

CAÇULINHA SUPERMARKET. Available at:

<https://www.empresascnpj.com/s/empresa/ribeiro-coimbra-cia-ltda-nome-fantasia-supermercado-caculinha/03222664000193>. Accessed on: September 4, 2017.

EXTRA SUPERMARKET. 2010. Available at:

<http://exame.abril.com.br/negocios/pao-acucar-inaugura-lojas-extra-assai-palmas-525588>. Accessed on: September 4, 2017.

MACRO SUPERMARKET. 2009. Available at: <http://conexaoto.com.br/2009/10/29/makro-inaugura-loja-em-palmas>. Accessed on: 08 Sep. 2017.

QUARTETTO SUPERMARKET. 2015. Available at: <https://www.quartetto.com.br/quem-somos>. Accessed on: 09 Sep. 2017.

TOLEDO, E. L.; VAZ, A. A. A. **Sales promotion:** a tool to encourage consumption. 2008. Available at: < https://www.insite.pro.br/>. Accessed on: September 9, 2017.

TRMNOS, A. N. S. **Introduction to research in the social sciences:** qualitative research in education. Sao Paulo: 1987.

VAROTO, L. F. **Ponto de vista:** retail history. FGV/EAES, Sao Paulo, v. 5, n. 1, feb./ apr. 2006.

WOILLER, S.; MATHIAS, W. F. **Projects:** planning, elaboration and analysis. Sao Paulo: Atlas, 1996.

APPENDIX

APPENDIX A - QUESTIONNAIRE

Questionnaire no. ( )

AGE:

SEX

PROFESSION:

PRAÇA

1)Is the location of a supermarket important to you?

2) Is it near your home or work?

3)Is it a decisive factor in your choice?

4) Does this supermarket have a parking lot? Is that important to you?

INTERNAL LAYOUT OF THE SUPERMARKET

1)   Do you find it easy to find the products you need on the supermarket shelves?

2)   Have you ever needed help to locate a specific product?

3)   Do you usually find queues when you go to pay? How do you feel about this?

PRODUCTS

1)   Do you always find what you need in this supermarket?

2)   Even the brands you want?

3)   Would you stop shopping there if your favorite brands weren't available?

4)   Do you think there is a variety of products in this supermarket?

SUPERMARKET PRICES

1)   Do you compare prices in this supermarket with others?

2)   Do you ever stop buying there because of the prices?

3) Have you heard any positive or negative comments about the prices in this supermarket?

PROMOTION

1)   Does this supermarket run promotions? If so, how do you find out about them?

2) Would you stop shopping there if another supermarket started offering better deals?

3) What kind of product would you most like to see on sale?

4) Have you ever gone to the supermarket because of a promotion and ended up buying other things?

SERVICE

1) Are the attendants/cashiers friendly?

GENERAL

1) In general, what do you think is important for a person to choose a supermarket?

2) What would make you stop shopping at that supermarket?

Printed by Books on Demand GmbH, Norderstedt / Germany